Med

Yeshigeta Mekuria

Medical Ethics & Professional Liability

Conceptual Foundations, Major Ethical and Legal Principles,Patient Physicians Relationship

LAP LAMBERT Academic Publishing

Impressum / Imprint

Bibliografische Information der Deutschen Nationalbibliothek: Die Deutsche Nationalbibliothek verzeichnet diese Publikation in der Deutschen Nationalbibliografie; detaillierte bibliografische Daten sind im Internet über http://dnb.d-nb.de abrufbar.
Alle in diesem Buch genannten Marken und Produktnamen unterliegen warenzeichen-, marken- oder patentrechtlichem Schutz bzw. sind Warenzeichen oder eingetragene Warenzeichen der jeweiligen Inhaber. Die Wiedergabe von Marken, Produktnamen, Gebrauchsnamen, Handelsnamen, Warenbezeichnungen u.s.w. in diesem Werk berechtigt auch ohne besondere Kennzeichnung nicht zu der Annahme, dass solche Namen im Sinne der Warenzeichen- und Markenschutzgesetzgebung als frei zu betrachten wären und daher von jedermann benutzt werden dürften.

Bibliographic information published by the Deutsche Nationalbibliothek: The Deutsche Nationalbibliothek lists this publication in the Deutsche Nationalbibliografie; detailed bibliographic data are available in the Internet at http://dnb.d-nb.de.
Any brand names and product names mentioned in this book are subject to trademark, brand or patent protection and are trademarks or registered trademarks of their respective holders. The use of brand names, product names, common names, trade names, product descriptions etc. even without a particular marking in this works is in no way to be construed to mean that such names may be regarded as unrestricted in respect of trademark and brand protection legislation and could thus be used by anyone.

Coverbild / Cover image: www.ingimage.com

Verlag / Publisher:
LAP LAMBERT Academic Publishing
ist ein Imprint der / is a trademark of
AV Akademikerverlag GmbH & Co. KG
Heinrich-Böcking-Str. 6-8, 66121 Saarbrücken, Deutschland / Germany
Email: info@lap-publishing.com

Herstellung: siehe letzte Seite /
Printed at: see last page
ISBN: 978-3-659-38084-6

St, Mary's UNIVERSITY COLLEGE

FACULTY OF LAW

MEDICAL ETHICS AND PROFESSIONAL LIABILITY

ADVISER: AMHA TESFAY (LLB), (LLM)

Submitted in Partial Fulfillment of the Requirement for the
Degree of Bachelor of Laws (LLB) In Faculty of Law St, Mary's University College

PREPARED BY YESHIGETA MEKURIA

July, 2007

1

ACKNOWLEDGMENTS

I am highly indebted to Dr, Yewondwosen Tadesse for meeting the many demands required for the preparation of this thesis. Dr, Koang Tutlam Deng, Dr, Fetih Yahya, Dr, Yared Mamushet, Dr, Dufera Mekonen, and Ato Wubetu Assefa, have shared me their precious time and expertise. W/o Tigist Hailu and Tsedale Leuelseged who skillfully carried out computer setting and Tibibe Sirak, whose in visionary ideas catalyzed the inception of this thesis My wife Hirut Leulseged ,my Colleagues Kidane Ayele and Shiferaw Gizaw for their kind encouragement to the successful completion of this thesis. And at last but not the least the most significant contributor, my advisor Ato Amha Tesfay who have endured , provided me books of medical laws ,related articles ,Knowledgeable advices ,edited and sustained me through out the preparation of this thesis .

TABLE OF CONTENT

Contents

CONCLUSION AND RECOMMENDATIONS...........................

Bibliography..64

INTRODUCTION

Back ground of the study

It is common knowledge, that every person who entered in to a learned profession is expected to the exercise of it at a reasonable degree of care and skill; however the nature, ethical and professional guiding principle and the extents of the duties of the professionals vary in different professions.

The medical professionals are duty bound to maintain ethics of the profession that the profession so require such as, the discipline of evaluating the merits, risks and social concerns of activities in the field of medicine. And also that has been enshrined in codes of professional ethics, ever since Hippocratic oath to date; including codes such as the first adopted in 1847 by the American medical association, the international code of medical ethics, the Geneva declaration.

Medical professionals failure to observe medical ethics i.e. the principles that doctor should consider in the performance of his professional obligation and in not exercising such prudence and skill as expected from an average member of his/her profession conformed to the method of doing things as to the expected standard. Results in economic loss, injury, and above all may cause death of individuals. This in turn, constitutes civil and criminal liabilities.

But, however there is legal remedy, it was observed that only few cases have been brought to court ever since the modern medicine introduced to our country, out of which only two decided cases have been used for the purposes of this thesis and there are cases pending, thus the suggested findings for the above stated facts are :-

- ➢ Lack of awareness of the victims, relatives and friends that the medical professional is liable for the negligent act/omission he/she commit in due course of their duty.
- ➢ Lack of the knowledge as regard to availability of methods to evaluate either the ethical situation are observed or not and that there are tests for negligent professionals.

Thus, this study mainly focuses to alleviate the problems of the breach of professional duties, and gearing the medical professionals to give at most attention to the medical ethics, in due course of performing their duty. And at times when failure to maintain professional obligations that the medical ethics so requires and causes damage, injury or loss of life to patients, the law it self regards professional liability so as not to leave the victim remediless.

This however may cause to dissuade talented individuals from entering to the profession by the threat of exposure to civil and criminal liability. Thus, solutions are sought which would take into account of this factors i.e. professional indemnity insurance concerned with the /liability of learned professionals/ for injury, damage, or financial loss will be discussed thoroughly.

The general objective of the study is to asses the ethical and legal aspects in the health care practice in Ethiopia.

> To create awareness for the public, i.e. the patient has the right to claim for injury damage or financial loss because of none observance of the ethical and professional duties of the medical professionals.

> To enlighten the legal professionals, that there are tests to determine the existence of negligence, E.g., Body of responsible medical men skilled in that particular art/. Or prudent patient test, i.e. methods of testing the existence of ethical situations

> To show that failure to maintain medical ethics entails professional liabilities to the medical professionals.

The findings of this study will be beneficial to alleviate the problems of breach of professional duty, that might have been caused due to none observance of medical ethics being seen often and also shows that there is possible remedy to the injured and there are civil and criminal liabilities for medical professional's act, error or omission. It furnishes as well information's to the medical professionals to have professional indemnity insurance so as not to leave the victim with out compensation.

The study explores the conceptual foundations of ethics and morality, the historical development of Ethiopian medical profession in the first chapter. The second chapter mainly deals with ethical and legal principles while the third chapter focuses on patient's right and professional obligation. the fourth chapter thoroughly, discuss on cases of breach of professional duty and liabilities of the medical professional's , decided and pending cases in the federal high court; and also ethical and professional guide lines of the ministry of health, the ethical curricula of the Addis Ababa University medical faculty and the Ethiopian medical association. Finally, chapter five is dedicated for the medical professional safe guard measure, conclusions and recommendations.

CHAPTER ONE Conceptual Foundations

1.1 THE CONCEPTS OF ETHICS AND MORALITY

It is of vital importance to look in to the etymological roots of the word ethics and the definitions set by different philosophers and scholars and how it has developed with societal development to have a clear understanding of the word "ethics" and "morality" so as to meet my purpose of studying medical ethics and professional liabilities.

Etymologically, the word "ethics" derived from the Greek ethos, in Homer's Iliad denoted a location, a place where people lived together. Through time, the word has acquired meanings that include custom, temperament, character and way of thinking.[1]

Thus the history of the word "ethos" could be realized that the customs and characters of men emerge in the course of their co existence.

Aristotle the great philosopher who studied the subject ethics formulated the adjective 'ethicos' based on the meaning of ethos as character (temperament), and as well he formulated the word 'ethica' to denote the discipline of ethical virtue.[2]

The Latin word for ethos is roughly 'mos' which can be translated as mores, custom, character, behavior, property inner nature, law, regulation style of clothing.[3]

Here we perceive that in essence the word ethics has similar roots as that of the Greek predecessors in the Latin of ancient Rome. Based on the Greek precedent having referred to Aristotle, Cicero formed the adjective moralis which pertains to (character, customs.) and later in the 4th century AD. Romans formulated the term moralitas. Etymologically, the Greek ethica and the Latin moralitas are the same.[4]

The two terms ethics and morality do have the common origin. Despite ethics and morality at times over lap as regards to their content is concerned, the term ethics has retained its original meaning and still denotes scientific discipline while morality is to be studied by it.[5]

Encyclopedia Britannica defines that:-

"Ethics is a branch of philosophy concerned with the nature of ultimate value and the standards by which human actions right or wrong. The terms also applied to any system or theory of moral values or principles." [6]

The term "morality" on the other hand used to refer to traditions of belief about right or wrong human conduct. Morality is a social institution in history. and a code of learnable rules that comes in to a picture only when certain things ought or ought not to be done because of their deep social importance in the way they affect justice these reveal that morality can not be purely a personal policy but rather by its very nature a social code.[7]

To summarize this analysis, however, terminological confusion have been observed, in everyday language, ethics is a scientific interest of the people i.e. avoiding harm, respecting others and observing the rules of discipline, while morality is its object. But to my purposes of studying medical ethics, the term "Ethics" would serve as general term referring to both morality and ethical theory as these terms are loosely interchangeable I may use the word ethics and morality interchangeably in my studying of the medical ethics and professional liability. For instance, legal ethics, ethical norms and medical ethics designate morality in abstract.[8]

1.2 Sources of medical ethics

Medical ethics emerged partially from concerns by physicians with etiquettes and such concern with etiquette goes back to the very beginnings of western medicine.

In the corpus, Hippocraticum as on respectability, and the Perivale's medical ethics codes of physicians. The American thought, such as, the 1st adopted by the American medical association in the year 1847. The International code of ethics, adopted by the 3rd general assembly of the world medical association in, London, England in. The declaration of Geneva adopted by the second general assembly of the world medical association, and amended by the 22nd world medical in assembly Sydney, Australia August 1968, and the national ethical and professional guide lines are notable sources of medical ethics. [9]

These codes of ethics ever since the Hippocratic Oath onwards to date, have been served as in providing standards of behavior and principles to be observed and as well they serve to promote ethical and professional guidelines that entail obligations i.e. Ideally the medical professionals are expected to give prompt response to the special needs of those who are ill to the best of their knowledge with at most due care, compassion, kindliness, promise keeping, confidentiality, autonomy and when found necessary to the best interests of the patient. [10]

Here one can perceive that the medical ethics rights and duties spells out obligations that out weigh than that of the traditional laws /law of tort, law of contract etc. / defines. [11]

However, each country adopts with certain modifications according to prevailing local culture religious beliefs, social norms and standards of medical practice, Ethiopia has her own modified codes of Ethics, that is expected to meet the countries present needs such as, Ethics for physicians practicing in Ethiopia. [12]

1.3 THE CONCEPTS OF PROFESSION

It is of paramount importance to define the term profession to provide sufficient analysis to my purposes of studying the medical profession. To this effect, it is important to see some of the definitions given by different authors.

As Roscoe described it so convincingly, it is that:-

"A group of men is pursuing a learned art in the sprit of public service"

According to Black's law dictionary:-

"Learned professions are characterized by the need of un usual learning, the existence of confidential relations the adherence to a standard of ethics higher than that of the market place, and in a profession like that of medicine by intimate and delicate personal ministration. Traditionally, the learned professions were theology, law and medicine, but some other occupations have climbed and still others may climb to the professional plane" [13]

Black's law defines the word professional as well:-

> *"A person who belongs to a learned profession or whose occupation requires a high level of training and proficiency"*

Concise law dictionary defines:-

> *"Profession includes vocation. The term is applied to an occupation or calling which requires learned and special preparation in the acquirement of scientific knowledge and skill"*[14]

> *"Professional means a person who is having special expertise in a field which would promote the wall fare of persons with disability"*

Thus, from the above definitions, we can perceive that the term Profession is a learned art acquired through learning that requires a high-level ethics and a high level skill obtained through high level training. In deed, it is different from ordinary occupation.[15]

The analogous term professional could be as well be defined as a person who is having a special expertise to provide his services to the wellbeing of the needy in a learned conduct, which entails professional duties.

When professional standards distorted and values of the profession are abandoned it affects a great deal the individual's work and the status of his professional colleagues too. And as well entails liability for failing to over come his obligation with due care and diligence.[16]

A Professional duty implies that individuals qualifications and competence up to a certain level makes him duty bound. to provide his services as to the member of that profession i.e. the law expects the professionals to perform their duties with standards of behavior and principles to be observed, and instill moral obligation to one another, to their clients and the general public.[17]

7

1.4 HISTORICAL DEVELOPMENT OF THE MEDICAL PROFESSION & THE MEDICAL LEGISLATION IN ETHIOPIA

Modern medicine introduced to Ethiopia by the first foreign practitioner Joao Bermudez a barber surgeon from Portugal, arrived with Portuguese embassy of 1520- 1526, during the reign of Emperor Libne Dingle. [18]

The then Ethiopian ruler, emperor Libne Dingle who was much interested in importing foreign medical skills had already written to king jao III of Portugal in 1521 asking him to send various foreigners including men who make medicines, and physicians and surgeons to cur illness. [19]

A century later German Lutheran missionary Peter Hailing, practiced medicine at the then new city of Gondor, besides practicing his physic" Hailing was also thought the children of the nobility that won the fever of Fasiladas 1632-1667. [20]

In 1698 he sent an agent Hajji Ali to Cairo with instruction to procure medical aid as Iyasu and his son both were suffering from a sever skin compliant. In response to his request the French consul in Cairo sent for Charles Jacques Poncet, arrived Gondor on July 11, 1699. Poncet prescribed to the emperor and his son and they begun their course of psych" and both observed exactly the dyet (regime) successfully cured in a little time [21]

Poncet was not described confined him self, Iyasu's illness, but Jams Bruce who visited Gondar three quarter a century latter reveled Poncet's two royal patients were suffering from "scorbutic" habit threatened to turn to leprosy. [22]

It can be realized that Poncet kept the secret of his patients i.e. (principle of confidentiality) may be with due consideration to the disease leprosy leaves social stigma against his royal patients by their subjects..

In the 1st decade of the 19th century the increased number of travelers, missionaries, scholars and diplomats' of different countries dabbled to a greater or lesser extent medicine. [23]

With the expanding of medical profession the number of Doctor's and Dentists grew significantly after world war I, and justified to the establishment of an Ethiopian medical

8

association in 1927 the year after that, it was reported that there were 25 physicians in the capital and six dentists in 1935.[24]

Apart from the development of the medical profession and the growing number of professionals, the establishment of the professional association evolved. The then Modern medical legislation enacted in July 18, 1930 was of the first attempt to put the medical and allied professions on a sound legal footing.[25]

The law placed the medical and allied professions under the supervision and control of the ministry of interior, accordingly medical doctors, Dentists, pharmacist, mid wives and veterinarian have to show their diplomas to that ministry with in three months after, to receive official authorization to practice.

The ministry was responsible to keep a register of practitioner, and the law was specified that no one could exercise these professions or run pharmacy without holding relevant diploma and persons who are failing to register and found practicing the medical profession were liable to a fine of from 20 – 2000 Eth. Birr depending on the gravity of the case. And a pharmacist for any contravention of the regulations rendered is liable to a fine 5 - 5000 Eth. Birr. The ministry had the power to withdraw the right to practice from any one who broke the law repeatedly.

As regards, to foreigners could elect as an alternative to receive penalties commensurate with those in the country.

However laws pertaining registration of the medical practitioners pharmacist and druggists were promulgated in 1942 and 1943 respectively, these laws was repealed and replaced by medical practitioners, pharmacist and druggists registration proclamation which was promulgated in1948, when the department of public health was made the ministry of public health.[26]

The proclamation pertaining drug administration and control, proclamation No 176/1999 that define the medical practitioners, powers and duties of the authority and offences related to drugs have been issued.[27]

Thereafter, the regulation regarding health professionals' council establishment Regulation no 76/ 2002.[28] that define the "Health profession", "Health institution", "Professional competence confirmation certificate", and as well that delineate the powers and duties of the councils executive committee, sub committee and of the Minster have been issued. From this, regulation articles found to be of greater significance to the purpose of this thesis extracted and summarized here under.[28]

According Art.15 of the regulation no 76/ 2002 the registration and professional license sub committee conferred with the power and duties:[29]

To verify applications and the documents attached therewith those submitted for registration, professional competence confirmation certificate and submit the result along with its opinion to the executive committee.

Set the criteria for a professional license of the respective standard and submit it to the executive committee.

Art. 16 of the regulation no 76/ 2002 endowed with the power and duties to the professional ethics committee:-[30]

To investigate complaints logged on the none observance of professional ethics and if found sufficient evidence to support the compliant submitted, the committee may instruct the professional against whom the compliant is logged to come up with a defense in one month time.

The committee is responsible to collect evidence that may help it to put into operation its power and obligations conferred in to it. After carry out the investigation on complaints brought against the accused professional, the statement of defense and evidence obtained there by i.e. findings along with the proposed punishment, shall submit to the executive committee.

Art.23 of the regulation No 76/2002 states that suspension or cancellation of professional license of any health professional who violates these regulations or directives on health professional ethics issued under these regulations shall be suspended or canceled depending on the case.[31]

Art. 24 (2) 0f the regulation empowered the minister *with discretionary power* to uphold the proposed decision or to render a different decision. Moreover, his decision is to be final with respect to cases reexamined by the appropriate sub committee for the second time. With out prejudice to Art, 23 of the regulation discussed above, Art.24 (4) empowered as well that the minister to cancel, the license based on the proposed decision submitted by the council and for reasons specified such as:[32]

- When the appropriate body makes the proof that, the acquired license is from fraudulent document.

- When the convicted health professional for a serious crime that shows that, he has no professional competence considered as an ethical health professional.

- If found to have been deliberately above ones capacity in breaching the health professionals ethics.

- If the health professional found to have been giving his services to earn an illegal benefit, and while suspended in contravention of a written notice and decision of suspension.

Besides, these medical legislatives Ethiopia has "Medical Ethics For Physicians Practicing in Ethiopia" whose drafting members formed by the ministry of health, for the first time that came in to being in 1988 GC.[33]

However, these laws are regulated there are no designed procedure on how the aggrieved individuals lodges their compliant to the council. Pertaining this matter and on ethical issues an interview was conducted with the current chairman of the Ethiopian medical association and the chairman of National ethics committee Assistant professor Dr. Yewondwosen Tadesse. The Ethics Committee is a subcommittee of the Health Professional Council, a body established by the Council of Ministers Regulation number 76/2002. The committee is working towards establishing a system, that can be used when allegations of ethical misconduct are brought against a medical practitioner. These include deciding on where in the health care hierarchy complaints may be seen e.g. at the level of the health institution, the woreda health bureau, regional health bureau, etc, the procedure for appeals, etc. The committee had examined only a few cases so far even without procedural rules but intends to broaden its activities once procedural rules are established. Another area the committee plans to work on soon is to create awareness about medical ethics to health professionals and the public at large.[34]

1.5 MEDICAL ETHICS AND THE LAW

As most scholars agree medical ethics is not a branch of medicine but a branch of ethics [35] where as, the law is from its inception meant for adjudicating conflicts in a way that to preserve the basic societal order. In converse, ethics has broad-spectrum effects on our day-to-day relations ships with others and on how our inner self-moral values and character to be expressed in action.[35]

It is a mistaken belief for some one to expect the law involve in such a situation, as the legal doctrines are quite permissive with regard to medical practice. As stated on bioethics, the law is not repository of our ethical standards and values even when the law is concerned with moral problems. For instance, a law abiding person is not necessarily morally sensitive and virtuous. Although, there are situations in which the legal doctrines limit the physician.[36]

The medical ethics is that an innate humanism with basic norm "do no harm'', acquired through interpersonal relations, that can be regarded as a component of moral progress.[37]

However the significant distinctions between the philosophy, function and power of law and medical ethics are available, it is the fact that court rulings determine the out come of a particular legal controversy.[38]

Legal codes sets a general standard of conduct which must be adhered to civil or criminal consequences may follow a breach of the standard and on the contrary an assertion of ethics which is not adopted in to law may be a major professional and moral guiding principle, even though it is unenforceable .[39]

Therefore, law and medical ethics are perceivable as disciplines with frequent brush in close contact yet each discipline has unique parameter and a distinct focal point. Both medical ethics and the law share the objective of creating and maintaining societal good and have a sympathetic link.[40]

END NOTES- CHAPTER ONE

1. Natalia Belskaya 'Ethics' (Moscow 1989) ,P5.
2. Ibid.
3. Supra Note 1,At 6
4. Ibid.
5. Encyclopedia Britannica
6. Supra Note 1,At 6
7. Tom L Beauchamp & Le Roy Walters Contemporary Issue In Bio Ethics 3rd Ed.(Belmont , California 1989) 1.
8. Medical Ethics For Physicians Practicing In Ethiopia 'General Code Of Ethics' 2nd Ed. (1992)P.3
9. Spiker And Engelhard, Jr. (Eds.) Philosophical Medical Ethics: Its Nature And Significance (1977) Vol. 3, P 3
10. Gillian M Lockwood 'Confidentiality' (Sept.2006) 25 Medical Education Resource Africa. P. 24
11. Edmund D Pellegrino 'The Virtuous Physician And The Ethics Of Medicine' In Tom L Beauchamp & Le Roy Walters Contemporary Issue In Bio Ethics 3rd Ed.(Belmont , California 1989) P.320
12. Supra Note 1at 276.
13. Ibid.
14. Richard Pankhurst 'An Introduction To The Medical History Of Ethiopia' (1990), P. 139
15. Ibid
16. Supra Note 14 At140
17. Ibid
18. Supra Note 14 At1 170
19. Supra Note 14 At1 210
20. Supra Note 14 At 242,
21. Supra Note 14at243 ,244
22. Supra Note 14at 218

23. Ibid

24. Ibid

25. Drug Administration And Control , Proclamation No 176 /1999, Negarit Gazette Year No .

26. Health Professional Council Regulation No 76 / 2002 . Negarit Gazette Year 8 No 13

27. Supra Note 28Art 15,16

28. Supra Note 28 Art 23,)

29. Supra Note28,Art24(2)

30. Supra Note 8

31. Interview With Dr Yewondwossen Tadesse Assistant, Professor Of internal Medicine , faculty of medicine A.A.U. 27 may2007

32. Howard Broody MD, PHD. 'Ethical Decision In Medicine' 2nd Ed.

33. Supra Note 11at 320

34. Supra Note 7at 36

35. Supra Note 7.At 37

36. Http //Depts. Washington .Edu./ Bioethics/ Topics Law .Html. 2/23/2007

CAHPTER TWO Major Ethical and Legal Principle

2.1 Ethical Principles

"Respect for autonomy, beneficence, and justice"

2.1.1 Respect for autonomy

Ethical principles are most often used frameworks and are the basis to obtain a reasoned approach to the series of problems that may take place in the medical profession and as well they provide a comprehensive guide line of medical ethics issues as a whole besides leaving a substantial room for judgment in specific cases.

According to Beauchamp, the three moral principles are In need as a framework of principle in bioethics. However, these principles are none hierarchical i.e. one is not ranked over the other. the moral principle, respect for autonomy, is of prime importance because the principle. The word "Autonomy", the ancient Greek legacy coined of two words where autos (self) and nomos (rule or law) refers to political self governance in the city state where as in moral philosophy personal autonomy referred as personal self governance, remaining free from dominating interferences by others, and free from ones own limitation of free choice signifies its priority .[2]

As most convincingly described in Kantian ethics: - *"Autonomous persons are ends in themselves, determining their own destiny, and are not to be treated merely as means to the ends of others"*[3]

Thus, Respect for patient Autonomy means respecting the decision making capacities of the patient i.e. patients have the right to refuse or choose their treatment.

To respect the autonomy of a person is appreciation of that person's capacity; viewpoint and the rights of individuals to hold certain views, to make voluntary choices to accept the treatment or not , and to take certain actions based on personal values and beliefs. [4]

The moral principle that we respect the autonomy of persons to determine their own destiny must accord them the moral right to have their own opinion and act upon them but those actions should not violate moral rights of others.[5]

The principle serves as basis to justify the right to make autonomous decision and also it covers to the extent of such as listening patient's questions carefully and to give answers with due respect in a detailed manner, but not in superior command approach. [6]

Thus, the relationship between patients and doctors requires that the patient should participate in any most important medical decision. To participate in decision means the patient should be informed, prior any medical intervention as for the nature of the treatment, its risks and benefits and possible alternative medical treatment as well as the patient must be given a chance to show up his free will whether to accept the treatment. These are the salient feature of informed consent.[7]

2.1.2 The principle of beneficence

The term "Beneficence" has extensive set of meanings that comprises the doing of good and the active promotion of good, kindness, charity[8] i.e. humanly serving others. But, in its narrower meaning beneficence requires us to abstain from injuring others and to allow others and promote their essential and justifiable interest .This principle comprises the four elements such as:[9-]

1. One ought not inflict evil or harm (a principle of none malfeasance),

2. One ought to prevent evil or harm

3. One ought to remove evil or harm

4. One ought to do or promote good

These elements can best be expressed as *"an act of benevolence that is over and above obligation,"* As quoted by Beauchamp Tom .L these four elements were suggested by William frankna. Despite, frankna puts the four elements hierarchically the obligation expressed in 1 may not always ought weigh those expressed in no (2) and (4) for instance, to save the life's of a dying patient by a blood transfusion justifies the inflicted harm of vein puncture on the donor. Therefore, in such a situation one is expected to prefer one alternative to another, to the best interest of the patient.[10]

Here we can perceive that the principle of beneficence obliged the doctor to abstain from intentionally inflicting injury others and to promote the essential and justifiable interests of others.

To cite non medical example that are not strictly analogous to the feature of the medical case, but found relevant to show up the significant deference's between the day to day business relations and the doctor's patient relationship that require to give at most attention to the best interest of the patient noted hereunder:

> *"The car sales man has a duty not defraud you or to lie about the car ; but he has no obligation to look out for your best interests if he sees you about to buy a car much more expensive than the one you really need he has no duty to point this out. The physician on the other hand, is expected under the contractual model to be an advocate to the patient's interests (in legal terms, the doctor – patient relation ship is a fiduciary one); the doctor's responsibility will be judged according to much stricter standards.''[11]*

Beneficence presupposes an obligation to weigh and balance benefits against harms. Thus, professionals should act in the best interest of the patient i.e. balancing benefits of treatments against the risk and cost.[12]

2.1.3 Justice

Justice– the concept of justice has been analyzed by deferent theorists in different ways i.e. Johns Rawls's A theory of justice which is of a Kantian tradition deontological theory that has won a wide audience in deontological ethics is that I found define best the notion of justice to the purposes of my thesis. [13]

Rawls has set two fundamental principles of justice the first requires that "each person be permitted to the maximum amount of equal basic liberty compatible with a similar liberty

17

for others." Secondly, he lay down that "once this equal liberty is assured in equalities in social primary goods e.g. Income, rights and opportunities are to be allowed only if they benefit everyone and only if everyone has fair equality of opportunity." For Rawls, social institutions justice needs to be in conformity with these two basic principles. [14]

Rawls analysis of justices gives a clue to come up to the commonest understanding of the notion justice. Despite, the concept of justice perceived differently by deferent theorists but the commonest least principle are, like cases should be treated alike or in other words equal ought to be treated equally and un equals un equally. [15]

Thus, on the basis the above stated pointes it can be asserted, that in whatever respects are under consideration if persons are equal in those respect they should be treated equally.

In this regard, the health professionals in due course of their professional obligations they have to perform as to what the law expects from them i.e. in the decision of in who gets what treatment. This is part of the Doctors duty of care to justify the best interests of the patient i.e. on whom that the burden of moral justification rests on. [16]

These ethical principles discussed above are of greater significant to guide doctors on what Principles ought to apply to a given situation. ,

Despite, the conflicting problems may arise with the noble sounding principle of respect of autonomy /consent/ and the principle of beneficence /best interests of the patient/ contradict each other. For example, Refusals of the treatment by the patient as in the Jehovah's Witness's refusals blood transfusions in life threatening cases .and cases of persons of diminished autonomy/ in competent patients the public health, or shortage of resources for which a patient can not afford could be justifiable to restrict exercises of patient autonomy severely. [17]

2.2 Legal principles

2.2.1 Informed consent

The term "informed consent", had not appeared in any of the literature until 1957, and discussion of the concept as it is on use presently, began only around 1972. Concomitantly, a revolution was occurring in the traditional conception of the patient physician relationship moved from narrow focus on the physician obligation to disclose information to the quality of the patient's or subject's understanding and consent.[18]

The root premise is the concept, fundamental in an American jurisprudence, *that is* * *the* True consent is apprehended in this case to be dependent upon the informed exercise of choice, and thus the information disclosed by a physician must assist the patient, to understand and accept treatment voluntarily and if remain un treated the results to happen.[19]

Based on the above stated fact we can perceive that disclosure in medicine serves as the instrument of getting patients to "consent" to what physicians wanted them to agree to in the beginning.

Consent is fundamental in the contractual model of doctor patient relation ship requires that the patient be participated in any major medical decision. To be participated expressively, the patient must first be given any information he needs about the risks and benefits of the medical treatment and whether any alternative treatment available.[20]

One of the reasons for informed consent is that the patient's involvement in the decision-making process, and final decision pertaining care must be voluntary. Consent obtained from coercion, fraud or misrepresentation is legally be considered as no consent at all. In addition, from ethical perspective consent found involuntarily does not provide moral authorization for treatment because it does not respect patient's autonomy. Rather it affects a great deal to one's own free choice.[21]

The very purpose of the duty to inform patients, and both patients right to know and the physician's corresponding duty to tell him are of paramount importance to preserve the principle of autonomy i.e. to honor a person's free choices.

---

* *'[e] very human being of adult years and sound mind has a right to determine What shall be done in his own body' ... "*

19

So long as informed consent viewed as right, rights can be voluntarily waived. Such a situation can take place when, if the patient knows he may ask question and make up his own mind, but says instead "you are the doctor you know what is best for me", he has voluntarily waived his right to informed consent.[22]

Presently, informed consent is a serious concern of the health professionals, but this how ever, not from ethical awareness on the part of physician's but has come to be a highly publicized lawsuit, in which physician did not obtain informed consent and patients suffered from the risk of the treatment are collecting compensation .

To summarize major points discussed above on informed consent.[23]

1. The basic rationale of informed consent is to preserve patient's autonomy, i.e. Free from limitation of one's own choice.

2. The physicians are duty bound to disclose information that the particular   patient would ideally require in order to obtain a reasoned choice. This depends in part on the patient's own values. It as well, includes the risks and benefits of the proposed treatment, and the risks and benefits of any alternative treatments.

3. As a right with in the doctor patient relation ship informed consent may be waived, the patient may choose not to be informed about some features of the treatment, or may choose to allow others to make the decisions for him.

4. Informed consent once given can be with drawn.

5. Emotional stress mental illness does not preclude the possibility of informed consent.

2.2.2 Consent and the law

Consent is the basis in patient doctor's relation ship and a key test of the degree to which patient autonomy i.e. the principle of autonomy on which the philosophical valid consent rests.[24] With any health care practice it is important that the patient has given valid consent before carryout any treatment or intervention. In order to be valid, consent must be given by a patient who is competent, informed and must be free from coercion and voluntarily given.[25]

As convincingly put in the American jurisprudence "every human being of adult years and sound mind has a right to determine what shall be done with his own body..." True consent to what happens to one's self is the informed exercise of a choice, and that entails opportunity to evaluate knowledgably the options available and the possible risks to be involved.[26]

Concerning to this matter an interview was carried out with Dr. Fetih Yahaya. Dr, of chiropractic medicine who practiced in the united states of America for not less than two decades. said that, it is the duty of the physician to provide consent form and to inform the patient as to the specific diagnosis and treatment risk benefit and if available alternative treatments for the patients seeking his medical assistance in converse, failure to produce valid consent form results in legal consequence.[27]

Negligence

Despite, the meanings of the term negligence is confusing because of its normal dictionary meaning 'carelessness' and the strict legal meaning of the word breach of any duty known to the law. Thus, for the purpose of this thesis I use the meanings of the tort of negligence i.e. a breach of a duty to take care which is recognized by law.

According To The Civil Code Of Ethiopia Art.2031 (2) Specify That

'He shall be liable where due regard being had to scientific facts or the accepted rules of the practice of his profession; he is guilty of imprudence or of negligence constituting definite ignorance of his duties'[28]

On the basis of this definition it is of vital importance to list the points on which a plaintiff must prove in order to sustain an action in negligence are stated here under.[29]

- ➤ the defendant owes him a duty care;
- ➤ the defendant is in breach of that duty;
- ➤ he(the plaintiff) has suffered loss or damage as a direct result of the breach ; and
- ➤ The loss suffered is not remote.

It is the fact that members of the medical profession owe a high duty of care to their patient's. Even though, the existence of the contractual relation ship between doctor and patient is not relevant. The doctor should under take a reasonable degree of care in the performance of his/her professional obligation as to any person who entered in to a learned art, besides the medical ethics that impose ethical duty to serve patients humanly.[30]

Patients need information when choosing whether to accept treatment for instance (An operation) or undergo a diagnostic test in particular they need the information about the nature of the treatment its benefits and risk and possible alternative treatments. Doctor's may be negligent in not giving the patient certain relevant information before the patient gives for the operation or procedure was very much a mater of professional judgment in the context of the doctor's relation ship with a particular patient

The legal requirement to inform a patient of risk benefits and alternative treatments relates to the prevention of negligence.

In this regard, to have the impression of the legal consequences of the legal principle consent I have forwarded here under the typical example the case of Sid away upheld in the House of Lords.

Legal case history

A. The case of Sidaway V. Board of governors of Bethlem Royal Hospital and the Maudsley Hospital and Ors(1984)= the question before the court of appeal was to what extent a surgeon had a duty to provide his patient with information relevant to a proposed operation .

The fact

Mrs. Sidaway suffered a pain in her neck and right shoulder as a result of an old injury the surgeon recommended an operation on her spine to which Mrs. Sidaway consented. The operation carried an inherent risk of damage of the spinal cord assessed at between 1% and 2% although the effects of something going wrong could range from the mild to the catastrophic; the operation proceeded and Mrs. Sidaway suffered serious impairment as a result.

The issue

The plain tiff's case was that she had not been adequately informed of the risks involved. Therefore, Mrs. Sidaway's central claim was for damages for negligence. The plaintiff how ever failed, there were no question that the surgeon was negligent in the performance of the operation.

The judgment

In the context of medical diagnosis and treatment, the law was content to adopt the standard of the ordinary skilled medical man. I.e. A test by responsible body of medical men What information should be disclosed by a doctor was very much a matter of professional judgment in the contexts of the doctor's relation ship with a particular patient. In this case, the surgeon had acted correctly. He had regarded the possibility of spinal cord damage as to remote to form any part of the basis of judgment by Mrs. Sidaway as to whether she should accept the treatment recommended by him the fact that in the event he had been proved wrong did not prove he was negligent. The House of Lords (1985) up held the decision. Legal liabilities.[31]

Pertaining to legal matters discussed above the Ethiopian penal law Art. 65 prescribe that:-

An act done in the exercise of professional duty is not liable to punishment
when it is in accordance with the accepted practice of the profession and the
doer does not commit any grave professional fault .
Nothing in this article shall affect civil liability.

Here, we can perceive that a doctor is not negligent. If he has acted in conformity to the method of doing things as to the expected standard from an average person of his /her profession i.e. With the practice accepted as proper by responsible body of medical men skilled in that particular art' this is termed as (test) after the relevant legal case. The alternative taste to the Bolam test is the prudent patient test, which is widely used in North America. This test requires Doctors to provide the amount of information that the prudent patient needs. In the issue of sidaway's judgment, the Bolam test was applied. ?????

B.   In Jones .v Manchester Corporation (1952). A patient died after Pentothal was injected while the patient was still under anesthetic. Here it was held that a liability existed.[32]

2.2.3 Implied consent

The situation in which consent can be implied and which courts have also recognized   two exceptions to the informed consent doctrine are :-[33]

1. In case of emergency situations where consent can not be obtained and where the patient's life would be at risk by waiting for consent, to save the life of that patient the physician proceed assistance under implied consent .[34]
2. When the physician has reason to believe that full disclosure would lead to severe emotional trauma, in such a situation the physician expected to show up the clear evidence that this will occur, not just a vague suspicion, for fear that this turn in to a loophole to justify a general policy of non disclosure.[35]

The patient is coming to Hospital or is admitted does not imply consent to any examination, investigation or treatment. Because, the consent of the patient is required by law for the person to be touched even when taking the pulse or examining his chest. Otherwise, it can constitute battery/assault. Nevertheless, if the doctor says "I would like to take your pulse" and the patient offers his wrist and sits quietly by the time the doctor taking his pulse, the patients implied consent said obtained by the patient's behavioral expression.[36]

If a competent patient says "there is no way you are going to take my pulse". It would constitute battery/assault/ if a doctor ignored this and took the persons pulse.[37]

2.2.4 Competence (capacity)

A patient must be competent (have the capacity) to give consent or refuse for an investigation or treatment he would undergo. For example, a patient with emotional stress, mental illness is unlikely to be competent to give consent to or refuse an operation to repair his/her fractured neck of femur.[38]

A person should not be considered as in competent (lacking capacity) for his/her makes unwise decision or against to his/her best interest. Such a situation might lead doctors to the law what is termed as "functional" approach i.e. Since capacity is function specific a person is not globally competent or in competent.[39]

Thus, it is to be noted, that only his/her competence is to the particular act. I.e. a patient may be competent to make a will but in competent to consent, or refuse consent to the particular operation. This requires doctors to asses patients' capacity by analyzing on how the decision is made i.e. mainly deals with the process on how the person come up to that particular decision ,but not on the decision it self.

In principle competence is that on which the primary decision making responsibility of the patient rests on. i.e. competent adults (adults with the capacity to con or refuse treatment) competent adult may refuse any, even life saving treatment. But, there are exception in common law countries for instance, Mental health act (1983);[40] a patient with

25

mental disorder may be treated for that disorder without consent i.e. there are situation when enforced treatment is to be administered. In such a case doctors should act in the best interest of the patient.

2.2.5 Incompetent patients

Patients who are incompetent to assume decision making responsibility are:-[41]

1. The unconscious patients
2. The child patient below the age of understanding

Prior assessment of patient's capacity is of vital importance so as to justify that the patient is competent or in competent so long as we have the developed legal analysis of capacity (competence) in Ethiopia. The legal analysis of competence is not well developed in the common law and therefore, follows philosophical literature in assessing capacity.

Three stage in assessing capacity

Comprehension and retention of information relevant to making the decision

Ability to believe this information (there is no delusion interfering with such ability)

Ability to weigh the information and make a decision

In those cases where patients are not capable to assume decision, making responsibility the socially designated next of kin and other close relatives should be allowed to speak for the patient in decision making. And doctors should act in the best interest of the patient; this requires professional judgment the legal test is Bolam (responsible body of medical opinion).[42]

To summarize patients to be considered incompetent are children under the age of comprehension, and in adults who are mentally retarded, or else so mentally compromised that they cannot understand reality and make rational judgments.

2.2.6 Confidentiality

The principle of medical confidentiality that has been enshrined in medical codes of ethics ever since the Hippocratic Oath[*] i.e. onwards including the international code of medical ethics, the declaration of Geneva and the national code of medical ethics prepared by the Ethiopian medical association and the like that instill honesty and trust in by patients is now fading away.[43]

Thus, as Mark Siegler described it, a 'decrepit' concept [43]. The rational he said 'decrepit' is that instead of perpetuate the myth of confidentiality and invest energy to preserve, it is better if the public and the profession devote their attention to determine which aspects of the original principle of confidentiality would be of greater significance.

In this respect the concept of medical confidentiality can be interpreted as the view that the information that a doctor found about a patient in due course of performing his professional obligation 'belongs' to, the patient and that the patient has the right to determine who has access to, such information and the physician is 'taking' history.

The contractual model of doctor and patient relationship makes doctor's duty bound to guarantee confidentiality /secrecy, discretion/ in return for the confidence and honesty of the patient.[44]

Patients may give information to doctors in the belief that doctors will keep confidential, if the doctor breaches confidentiality, the patient may feel that the doctor has broken an implied agreement to keep his secret.[45]

Failure to observe confidentiality may cause serious consequences i.e. if patient discovers breach confidentiality he/she may loose trust in that particular doctor or doctors in general. If the complaints of breach of confidentiality have come to the knowledge by many people,

---

[*] *"what ever… I see or hear in the life of men, which ought not to be spoken of abroad, I will not divulge, as reckoning that all such should be kept secret"*

it may cause degradation of the public confidence towards the medical profession, resulting gross loss of trust and a serious unwanted effect on the health service activity.[46]

In medical confidentiality, there are situations in which doctors must not breach and there are situations, in which disclosure of patient's information /breach confidentiality/ by doctors may be justified in the public interest. Where failure to do so may expose the patient or others the risk of death or serious harm, i.e. if the risk is presumably outweigh the patient's privacy. In addition, a situation in which doctors discretionary power to breach of confidentiality stated here under:-[47]

A. Situations in which doctors must not disclose patient's information (breach of confidentiality).

Doctors should not write a report or fill in a form disclosing confidential information (eg, for an insurance company) without the patients consent (preferably written).[48]

Doctors working in sexually transmitted clinics – no information that identify a patient examined or treated for any sexually transmitted diseases should be provided to a third party (except in a few specific situation).[49]

To prevent minor crime, or to help conviction in minor crime (most crime concerning property are minor crimes in this context.)

'Casual breaches' (eg. for amusement, to satisfy another person's curiosity, by failure to anonymize in respect of details in reports or publications.

In This, Respect The Ethiopian Penal Code Art. 399 . Breach Of Professional Secrecy. Spells Out That

(d) *Doctors, dentists pharmacists midwives and auxiliary medical personnel, who disclose a secret that has come to his/her knowledge in the performance of his/her professional obligation even if the duties completed at the time of disclosure.*

And also the medical ethics for physicians practicing in Ethiopia imposes duty on physicians as stated here under:[50]

> *Art. 20 The physician to maintain the professional secrecy that has come to his knowledge in the course of his duties except in those situations clearly stipulated by the law or the patient gives written consent for the release of information.*

Brief comparative study of the breach of the law confidentiality , the proponent example of common law follower countries. United Kingdom. Vs. Ethiopia, the civil law follower country. (Lawful disclosure of patient's information)[51]

The issue of the law of confidentiality when it is lawful, and when not lawful for a doctor to breach confidentiality is often is a question of balancing public interest. Situation in which breach of confidentiality to be observed, both in our codes of law /Ethiopian/. And of the common law Acts, are separately described here under:-

B. Situations in which, doctors must disclose patient's information.

Examples of the law in UK, [52]	Examples of codes of law in ETHIOPIA, [53]	
➢ Notifiable diseases – public health (control disease.)		Art, 400 authorized disclosure,
	(1)	Any disclosure made especially in court or on the occasion of a dispute relating to insurance or compensation, shall not be punishable;
➢ Drug addiction-misuse of drugs Act (1973)	(a)	Where it is made with the express consent of the person interested in keeping the secret;
➢ Termination of pregnancy –Abortion Act (1967	(b)	Where, at the suggestion or request of the possessor of the secret, the competent higher professional or supervisory body has given its written permission for disclosure.
➢ Births – Births and deaths registration Act (1953)	(c)	Where it is made following an express and reasoned decision of a court of justice in a specific case;
➢ Deaths- Births and Deaths registration Act (1953)	(d)	Where special provisions of the law impose the duty in the interests of the public order. To give evidence before a court of justice to inform a public authority
➢ To police request name and address but not clinical details of driver of vehicle who is alleged to be guilty of an offence under the road Traffic Act. (1988)	(2)	Where disclosure is expressly ordered by law, by court of justice or by competent authority, the possessor of the secret can not invoke his professional obligation to maintain secrecy. Eth. penal code.
➢ Under court order		Art. 535. Required formalities and penalties for

Examples of the law in UK, [52]	Examples of codes of law in ETHIOPIA,[53]
	non observance.
➢ *Identification of donors and recipients of transplanted organs –Human organ transplant Act.(2000)*	*(1) The doctor who confirms the state of health justifying the termination of the pregnancy and authorizes the intervention shall keep a duplicate of the findings and decision and transmit them to the competent official department with in the period of time fixed by law. The doctor terminating the pregnancy shall notify that department forth with.*

Despite, there is general obligation for doctors to keep secrets of patients, as has been stated in Art. 400 of the penal code of Ethiopia, there are laws that allow breaches of confidentiality and there are situations, which obliges doctors to disclose patient's information. In both these situations, it is important that the doctors breach confidentiality only when the law requires, to the relevant person or authority, in a broad sense to the public interest.

C.   Situations in which doctors have discretion to disclose patient's information

➢ Sharing of information with other members of the health- care team in the interests of the patient

➢ A patient who is not medically fit to drive continues to do so, i.e. against the medical advice.

➢ A third party is at significant risk of harm. (Eg, partner of HIV positive person).

If we read each articles of the Ethiopian penal code which enlists laws regarding secrecy and analyze it thoroughly we can perceive that it is exactly resemblance to that of the common law Acts, discussed above pertaining laws of the principle of confidentiality.[54]

2.2.7 Truth Telling

The patient must tell the truth regarding to his medical condition, and has a right to participate in decision that are morally significant for him. This in turn calls for doctors what to tell the patient especially when one who is in terminal case or fatal illnesses.[57] In this respect what is expected of doctors in the decision making process is described under the title 'doctor and patients relationship' in the book of ethical decision in medicine.

> *"The physician should tell the patient the truth*
> *about his condition in language he can understand,*
> *unless the physician has reason to believe that the*
> *degree of harm, more serious than merely a*
> *temporary emotional depression, would follow as a*
> *result"* [55]

In such a situation to justify telling the truth or not to tell to a patient is rests on the doctor. Thus, if a doctor found that to tell the truth to the patient outweighs he must think of that it may last over a certain period of time but not a single time affair.

Thus, the mode of expression to be used whether to tell the truth all at once or little by little requires the doctor's ethical decision. In this regard to 'tell' or "not to tell" a decision in terminal illnesses requires an ethical judgment in itself. For instance if a physician tells the patient straightforwardly and then with draws with out offering any emotional support and the kind of follow up to help the patient and resolve his feelings, so as not to produce un wanted effect is un ethical.

32

In spite of the fact that it requires to be skilled at the science of human behavior before he decides to tell him, he needs to be first of all attentive listeners before he decides what to tell the patient, and how to .o it in the most humanly manner.

So far, we have discussed about terminal cases, but in converse, there are cases where 'bare faced lie' is used in the best interest of the patient.

For example, a treatment called "placebo" when pharmacologically inactive treatment has been given under the guise of active medicine i.e. such as substituting distilled water for a potent medicine much more likely to cause addiction, as well as it is believed that they are beneficial on psycho logic and hypochondria symptoms. So long as 'placebo' violates the general rule of telling the truth to patients it is not advisable to use it unless strongly justified.[56]

2.2.8 Professional codes of ethics

The rationale behind for the needs of professional codes could logically be assumed that those who can do something and others can not are immediately faced with definite responsibilities before the people using their services. Typical example to this statement is that of the ethical principle started with the codes of laws of Hammurabi (1790 B.C) under which the Babylonian surgeons were rewarded or punished for the results of their efforts./[57]

The first oaths of loyalty to a profession were evolved by a people who were humanly serving others was the oath taken in ancient Greek by the graduates of Aesculapius school, Evolved the ideas of the famous Greek physician who is regarded as the father of modern medicine Hippocrates. ever since, Hippocratic Oath to-date, professional oaths have been publicly and solemnly pledged by physicians as they are admitted to the medical profession, codes such as the first adopted in 1847 by the American medical association, the American Nurse association "code for nurses"(1976) , the international code of medical ethics, revised and updated codes of the (4th century B.C) Hippocratic Oath as the declaration of Geneva which adopted by the second general assembly of the world medical association, Geneva, Switzerland.[58] Appendices.

Of which Ethiopia adopts and has equal footing as to the law of the country according to art. 13 (2) of the FDRE Constitution and the medical ethics for physicians practicing in Ethiopia. Are of greater significant to keep up the standards of the services of the professionals.[59]

These professional codes of ethics provides, standards of behavior and principles to be observed and upholds the moral prestige of professional groups in society, instill confidence/[60] in them and imposes professional obligations with in the professionals them selves, their patients and the society as a whole.

Each and every professional medical codes discussed above entail obligations related to the special professional tasks of physicians in society, to observe the laws of the land, then observance of rights and fulfillments of duties, and finally the practice of virtue i.e. ideally the virtuous person is considered to do the right and the good.[61]

Medical professionals' failure to observe the professional codes of ethics i.e. the principles. That, doctors should consider in the performance of his professional obligation. and in not exercising such prudence and skill as expected standard results in, economic loss, injury and above all deaths of individuals, which constitutes civil and criminal liabilities under the law of the land and on the convention Ethiopia ratified evidencing the available methods that lend a hand us to evaluate the medical codes of ethics of a situation .

END NOTES- CHAPTER TWO

1. Tom L Beauchamp & Le Roy Walters Contemporary Issue In Bio Ethics 3rd Ed. (Belmont , California 1989) 30

2. Ibid

3. Supra Note 1 At 29

4. Ibid

5. Ibid

6. Ibid

7. Howard Broody MD, PHD. 'Ethical Decision In Medicine' 2nd Ed. (Boston, USA), 37

8. Ibid

9. Supra Note 1 At 30

10. Ibid

11. Ibid

12. Supra Note 7 At 63.

13. Supra Note 1 At 26

14. Supra Note 1 At 33

15. Supra Note 1 At 29

16. Ibid.

17. Supra Note 1 At 374

18. Supra Note 7 At 59

19. Presidents Commission For The Study Of Ethical Problems In Medicine And Biomedical And Behavioral Research Informed Consent As Active Shared Decision Making In. Tom L Beauchamp & Le Roy Walters Contemporary Issue In Bio Ethics 3rd Ed. (Belmont, California 1989) 390

20. Ibid

21. Supranote 7at 62

22. Supra Note 7 At 71

23. Tony Hope 'Valid Consent An Ethical Analysis' Medical Education Resource Africa (September2006)14

24. Ibid.

25. Spotswood W. Robinson, III 'Informed Consent' In Tom L Beauchamp & Le Roy Walters Contemporary Issue In Bio Ethics 3rd Ed.(Belmont , California 1989) 384.

26. Interview With Dr Fetih Yahaya Dr, Chiropractic Medicine (21 April 2007)

27. Allan J Peck, 'Legal Liabilities' The Chartered Insurance Institute (1991chatamp,Kent)1/5

28. Supra Note 7 At 64

29. Supra Note 23 At17

30. Ibid.

31. The Criminal   Code Of Federal Democratic Ethiopia Proclamation No.414/2004   Negaret Gazette, (2005) Art.69

32. Supra Note 27 At 10/8

33. Supra Note 7/64

34. Supra Note 23 At 17

35. Ibid.

36. Ibid

37. Ibid

38. Ibid

39. Ibid

40. Supra Note 7 At 111

41. Ibid

42. Mark Siegler 'Confidentiality In Medicine – Decrepit Concept' In Tom L. Beauchamp & Le Roy Walters Contemporary Issue In Bio Ethics 3rd Ed. (Belmont, California 1989) 405

43. Ibid

44. Supra Note 7at 53

45. Gillan M Lockwood 'Confidentiality' Medical Education Resource Africa (September 2006) P, 25

46. Ibid.

47. Ibid

48. Ibid

49. Supra Note 31at Art. 399

50. Medical Ethics For Physicians Practicing In Ethiopia 'General Code Of Ethics' 2nd Ed.(1992) Art.20

51. Supra Note 45 At 26

52. Supra Note 31 Art. 400

53. Supra Note 45 At 26

54. Supra Note 7at 49

55. Supra Note 7 At 52

56. Natalia Belskaya 'Ethics' (Moscow 1989) P 271

57. Ibid.

58. Supra Note 1 At 320

CHAPTER THREE Patient Physicians Relationship

3.1 The relationship between patients and the medical professionals

The primary ethical obligations of the health professionals rests on the relation ship between physicians nurses and the patients seeking their assistance, it is not the only possible means to the ethical evaluation of the patient professional relationship.[1]

In this regard, to look in to Edmund's recommendation of the "three stands" by which professionals behavior might be judged.[2] I have chosen the two i.e. one and three amongst the 'three stands' he identified, for their practical significance to this thesis are:-

b. Has he professionally violated any legal rules or administrative regulations in his/her treatment of the patient.[3] The standard to evaluate professional performance on the basis of its conformity with widely accepted ethical principles and moral rules such as the principle of autonomy of persons, confidentiality etc.

c. He stated as the third and stringent standard is that one that requires professionals not only to full fill their moral obligations, but the professionals to be virtuous and to perform morally right actions for the right reasons as an expressions of his/her concern for the wellbeing of others.[4]

In general to maintain the relationship between the health professionals themselves and more over with patients whose wellbeing is to be determined by these professionals, most importantly the professionals are expected to perform their duties as to the required standard, ethical obligations and responsiveness to the patient special needs with some degree of sympathy.

3.2 Patient's Right

In order to have a clear understanding of patient's right. It is of vital importance to define, what the legal term 'right' is and which rights of the patient are susceptible to violation.[5] To answer these questions, different philosophers have given the meanings they belief that sufficiently explain the term right and its function how ever they can not give mathematical answer to it. The definition forwarded by the philosophers provides us to analyze the legal concept broadly and find out the closest definition to the concept right.

In this respect, though there are many literatures on rights are available in archives of philosophy and jurisprudence. I have chosen the recent thoughts of john Rawls and Dowrkins.

To begin with john Rawls a theory of justice (1971) he put forward the two principles:-[6]

➢ Each person shall enjoy the most extensive liberty compatible with a like liberty for others.

➢ In equalities in wealth and power should exist only where they work to the benefit of the worst of members of society

From these premises, I perceive that the patient has the right to get services be it in what ever socio economic status i.e. desperately poor or well to do, so long as he needs treatment or professionals humanly assistance and the hospital must provide reasonable response to the request of a patient for services with in its capacity to preserve the persons natural right i.e. Such rights that are set out in the universal declaration of human rights (UDHR.) Art. 25 Which Ethiopia is a party to it states that:-[7]

> Every one has the right to a standard of living adequate for the health and well being of himself and of his family, including food, clothing housing and medical care and necessary social services, and the right to security in the event of an

39

employment, sickness, disability widowhood, old age or other lack of lively
hood in circumstances beyond his control. [8]

Ronald Dworkin in his book of essay "taking rights seriously" Dowrkin proposed that:-[9]

In most cases when we say that someone has right to something we imply that it would be wrong to interfere with his doing it or at least some special grounds are needed for justifying an interference.

In this regard the declaration of Lisbon, Portugal. On the rights of patients (1981) which adopted by the world medical association pertaining the rights of the patient provides that:-

The patient has the right to be cared for by a physician
Who is free to make clinical and ethical judgments without any out side
interference. [10]

Here we can conclude that patients right can not be interfered in any way without justifying the reason to his best interest as has been discussed under the title beneficence, or he himself voluntarily waived his right to informed consent i.e. the patients relying up on the physician professional competence and very high moral standard saying that you are my doctor and you know what is best for me.

3.3 Duties of the physicians

In the contractual relation of the physician and the patient, the physician has no obligation to cure the patient, but to exercise with due care that meets the standard meaning care that should not be below the care that would be shown in the circumstances by a reasonable careful physician. Deviation from professional standard is to be considered as fault in the practice of medicine, this criterion of negligence is a so called objective one.[11]

It means that the conduct of a physician is compared not with that specific person but with the model (the so called bonus medicus) or standard of the prudent and competent physician. The enquiry is what would have been if a prudent and competent physician in a given specific circumstances perform such a duty.[12]

Here it is to be noted that the test for the existence negligence is the conduct of the prudent, diligent and ordinary member of that profession.

The physicians can not guarantee that the contemplated objective will be attained. In respect to this although, Ethiopia doesn't have medical law it civil code specifies that under Art.2648, guarantee of cure :-

> *A physician shall not guarantee the success of his treatment unless he has expressly assumed this obligation in writing .[13]*

But the physicians how ever, they shall not guarantee to cure it is to be noted that they are duty bound to act diligently and prudently in conformity with the data and advances of the medical science. In other words the physicians are under obligation to use reasonable care and skill to perform their duties in accordance with the practice.

In converse the physician has no obligation to cure the patient means that he has no obligation to achieve a specific result, i.e. it is very difficult to expect physicians to guarantee the contemplated goal will be reached.

> *He can not compel nature goal attainment depends on the physician constituents and reaction of the patient .[14]*
> *A physician is generally un able to rely on scientific facts and calculations likely to assure complete certainty and safety .*

Factors influencing the physicians act should be of thought as neither the human body nor the human mind function according to the fixed rule.[15]

In contrast, courts have made exceptions to the rule, where the physician uses a known treatment of which out come is certain. The elements of uncertainty may be absent.

These are situations in which the physician may be obliged to achieve a specific result, if contaminated blood transfused; in accuracy of laboratory tests; or a defective appliance used by a dentist. In such a case a medical professional is liable for failure to achieve specific result in this kind of subsidiary duties.[16]

END NOTES- CHAPTER Three

1. Tom L Beauchamp & Le Roy Walters Contemporary Issue In Bio Ethics 3rd Ed.(Belmont , California 1989) 307

2. Edmund D Pellegrino 'The Virtuous Physician ,And The Ethics Of Medicine' In Tom L Beauchamp & Le Roy Walters Contemporary Issue In Bio Ethics 3rd Ed.(Belmont , California 1989) 320

3. Ibid

4. Ibid

5. Jeorge J. Annas 'The Emerging Stow Away Patients Right In The 1980s' In Tom L Beauchamp & Le Roy Walters Contemporary Issue In Bio Ethics 3rd Ed.(Belmont, California 1989) 336

6. Ibid.

7. Ibid.

8. Ibid

9. UDHR.Art 25

10. Jeorge J. Annas. Supra Note 5

11. Medical Ethics for physicians practicing in Ethiopia 'general code of ethics' 2nd ed. (1992) 34

12. International Encyclopedia Of Medical Law 165 (1997)

13. Civil Code Of Ethiopia Proclamation No. 165 Of 1960 Art.2648.

14. International Encyclopedia Supra Note 12at162

15. Ibid

16. Ibid

CHAPTER FOUR Professional Obligations

4.1 PROFESSIONAL LIABLITIES

The term 'professional liabilities' used in this thesis signify the responsibilities of the members of the medical profession in due course of exercising their profession.[1]

This applies for both diagnosis and treatment and also professionals are duty bound to know when one is out of one's depth and when to refer patients to a more imminent person in the field.[2]

In general both the law and the profession owes to the medical professionals to exercise a high duty of care to their patients and also the doctors must apply the ordinary degree of professional skill and follow approved practice. For not exercising such duty of care and prudence, what the law requires from an average member of the profession brings about professional liability (civil and criminal liabilities).

In Ethiopia the 'professional liability' has not been governed by a special law i.e. medical law, which is a recent development in countries like Belgium, UK and USA which now a days considered as a subject in its own right and in service as regards to the medical professional liability. But in Ethiopia, both civil and criminal liability of the physician for damage or injury caused by improper performance of their duties in the discharge of his/her professional obligations are governed by the traditional civil and criminal law as the rest of the world were using it before the development of medical law of to date.[3]

It is very recently that the enlightened patient's relatives have started to claim against the medical professionals and there fore the number of cases brought before the court were very minimal indeed i.e. only two decided cases I found on which I will discuss here under briefly.

44

To this effect, how ever there are factors presumably influencing for the patients to bring their case to court i.e. lack of awareness, fear for the absence of witnesses to the individual patient claim and believing doctors are virtuous (perform their duties humanly). But it is foolish to think that the physicians never and ever commit or omit and as well only these two cases appeared to court were entailed professional liability in the past years, in spite of the fact that the are no cases reported on law journals and the lesser the effort done on my part to search for it.

4.2 CIVIL LIABLITIES of physicians

A civil liability of physician arises when an obligation is not fulfilled. Obligations emanates either from contract or from tort.

In this regard the Belgian courts the proponents of the French jurisprudence which is the same as to how our courts do have recognized the possibilities of contract for medical services existing between physician and his patient or between the employer of the physician and in most cases the hospital and patient.

However, the existence of a contractual relation ship between doctor and patient is not relevant. Because, if a physician causes personal injuries through malpractice, not only breaches his contract but also commits a tort the problem of such kind as to whether proceed in contracts and or in tort have been resolved by a decision of the court of cassation of 7 December 1973 that excludes the so called concurrent or alternative liability.

Therefore, the non contractual or tortuous liability is only relevant in the case of damage to a third party or where services are rendered to a patient when the patient is not in a position to give consent to treatment and the professional .

According to the said land mark decision of the French court of cassation of 20 may 1936. Stated here under:-[3]

"*The contract between the physician and his patient results in*

45

an obligation not to cure the patient but to offer him medical help consicientiously and diligently in conformity with the data and advances of medical science"

Therefore, this can be interpreted in a way that the physician has no obligation to achieve specific result but an obligation to use reasonable care and skill. In this regard the Ethiopian law of extra contractual liability on Art. 2031 As regards 'professional fault' prescribes that:-

> *(1) A person practicing a profession or a specific activity shall in the practice of such profession or activity, observe the rules governing that practice.[4]*

Here we can perceive that Ethiopian law regarding to the professional fault is exactly the same as to that of the laws of the followers of the French jurisprudence and there fore this sub article (1) of 2031 could serve to invoke at times when the medical professionals fail to meet the standard /observe the rules governing that practice/ with out undergoing to analogy.

> *(2) He shall be liable where due regard being had to a scientific fact or the accepted rules of the practice of his profession; he is guilty of imprudence or of negligence constituting definite ignorance of his duties.[5]*

In this regard the Belgian law which is of French origin like ours clarify the causes of negligence as deviation from the professional standard as compared with the model (the so called bonus medicus) or standard of the prudent and competent physician. If a physician that does something a physician of ordinary prudence would not do. He is negligent.

Thus, however the sentences are set out differently with that of our law Art.2031 (2) its meaning and implications are the same with the Belgian law stated here above.[6]

46

4.3 Criminal liability

In due course of performing his duty a physician may cause bodily harm to the patient and this consequently qualified as criminal act. according to Art 23 (1) of the penal code of Ethiopia i.e. for an act of commission or omission in other wards to do an act what the laws prohibit not to do and not to perform an act what the law so requires to perform are shall be punishable. Thus, the professional has to act as to the standards that the profession requires diligently.

In this regard the Ethiopian penal code Art 69 of the 2005 as amended, prescribes that ;-

Art.69- professional duty.

> *An act done in the exercise of a professional duty is not liable to punishment when it is in accordance with the accepted practice of the profession and the doer does not commit any grave professional fault.*
>
> *Nothing in this article shall affect civil liability.* [7]

And if any deviation from, also a minor one of the professional standard that causes bodily harm to the patient is criminally punishable.

Damages

The legal term damages are confusing to non-member of the legal profession. Thus, it is pretty fair to clear the misunderstanding between the words "damage" and "damages" for which the former refers to an injury causing a loss to the persons interests. these are mainly of two kinds: material or moral harm to a person's material interest that affects "his material wealth" and Harm to his moral interest affects his internal feelings, while the latter term damages means to redress i.e. compensation awarded to remedy the injured. [8]

Here, we can realize that where there is damage that damages to be anticipated. Hence, these two terms exemplified, as damage is the cause and damages as its effect.

In principle all the damage the patient suffered has to be compensated, including the different sorts of moral damage. Nevertheless, a patient is only entitled to recover damages in respect of negligent medical treatment if he has actually suffered damage. [9]

47

In this respect the Ethiopian civil code Art.2650 imposes liability on physician to third parties at times when the physician causes loss of death to individuals by his own fault.10

To this effect Art. 2650(2) specifies that : -

> *Compensation shall not due because of moral loss suffered by*
> *these persons unless the death of the sick person has been due*
> *to the intentional act of the physician.*

As regards to the moral harm for not to be compensable the Ethiopian law has a resemblance to that of the medical law of Belgium, except in that our law concerns mainly with the intentional act of the physician for the moral harm to be compensated.

A Physician is liable :- according Art.2650 (1)

> *In the case of mortal accident due to the fault of the physician the*
> *husband or wife of a sick person or his ascendants or descendants*
> *may claim from the physician compensation for the loss which they*
> *have suffered through the sick person.*[11]

Despite, we have laws that provides the injured to be compensable for the damage he/she suffered and however not few cases appeared to court there was no case in which the civil suit raised let alone to seek a remedy for the damage they sustained.

As regards the rights of the claimants Art.2650(3) stats that:-

> *No other person may claim compensation in their own right by reason of the*
> *death of the sick perso ,not withstanding that they are able to prove that the*
> *letter rendered them material assistance or that they were maintained by him.*[12]

4.4 Causation

Causation is highly relevant in cases of medical negligence is that, in order to succeed in an action in tort the plaintiff must also show that the injury has been proximately caused by the defendants lack of care.[13]

The onus on the plaintiff to show causal connection between breach of duty of care and damage.

As in cases of the medical practice the poof of the plaintiff is not only limited to show up that the defendant physician was negligent but also that the defendant's negligence was the cause of the damage he has sustained

Many injuries how ever result from complex of events and possible causes that require to be examined whether there was un broken sequence of events between the original act of negligence and the resultant loss in other ward when the cause and effect was not terminated then the plaintiff could recover that loss.[14]

I t is paramount importance to cite medical example of such a situation involved in the court battle of Tesfaye VS. professor Taye.[15] After the professor performed his operation and went home while seeing the operated patient suffering from sever pain the professor's assistants were opened once again the patient's abdomen and withdrew three liters of blood to relieve him from sever pain he was suffered from, this fact was led the court to frame issue whether the cause and effect terminated because of the second operation or not was the issue of causation which latter resolved .see appendices.

4.5 Vicarious liability

Vicarious liability is by definition liability for the wrong full acts of others with out ones own fault i.e. acts or omission . If that is the case physicians are liable for the negligent acts or omissions of the employee he employs to assist him perform his own duties it means that he will be liable for the wrong full acts of his staff.[16]

When a physician works in a hospital on the basis of so called contract of admission and makes use of personnel and services provided to him by the hospital , Pertaining to this matter the Ethiopian civil code has clearly setout that Hospitals are liable for the acts of their medical staff, though, its practical applicability have not yet been seen . As regards to the liabilities of the hospital Art. 2651 of the Ethiopian civil code , liability of medical institution- 1 medical treatment.

The medical institution shall be civilly liable for the damage caused to a sick person by the fault of the physician or auxiliary staff which it employees.[17]

Amongst , the various causes that involve medical mal practice, because hospitals are using sophisticated diagnostic and therapeutic apparatus are available, the use of which requires specific skill and care that call for actions based on the use of defective equipment and claims with respect inexpert use of available apparatus and or lack of supervision on the technicians using this apparatus and also no use was made of a piece of equipment even if it is available and in good shape at the time.[18]

Though the law makes medical institutions vicariously liable for the damage caused by their employees, the practice is not yet developed.

To cite a few example here under case analysis was made possible in the case Tesfaye vs. professor Taye and in the case frehiwot vs. Dr. Ashagare in both case the hospital was vicariously liable if the case would have been brought to court.

50

Case analysis

In the case of Tesfaye Beza vs. professor Taye mekuria

Tesfaye Beza 50, on the 26th of Meskerem 1985 EC. went to Zewditu Hospital for the first time with the compliant of right upper quadrant abdominal pain, The pain was thought to be caused by gall bladder wall inflammation /mass/ as identified by the ultrasound examination, but gall bladder stone was not seen.

And also he under went X ray and laboratory examination and the results were found to be in normal limit.

After the examination done by internist, Tesfaye was referred to the surgeon professor Taye.

On the 12, January 1985 the professor himself examined and told the patient to be hospitalized, fallowing his order on the 7th march 1985 Tesfaye admitted to Zewditue hospital, and the operation was performed on the 9th march 1985 E.C. Soon after the operation the patient's abdomen became swollen and when other doctors saw his suffering opened his abdomen and withdrawn 3 (three) liters blood and stitched. Nevertheless, they have made efforts the patient died. The case went to the federal high court.

The issue

The central claim of the prosecutor was that the defendant having known the reason for such a case is a chronic liver diseases, and if the gall bladder removed that it causes sever bleeding and death, he had removed the gall bladder imprudently and negligently that resulted in to the patient's death, in disregarding to Art.526 (2) of the penal code of Ethiopia.

The judgment

The legal issue at the crux was that is it usual practice for a surgeon to remove shrank gall bladder having seen a liver is shrank too? And did the patient get proper care that meets the professional standard. Is the defendant /surgeon/ responsible for follow up and care after he performed surgery. The report from the body of the medical professionals committee formed by the ministry of health and physically appeared medical professionals testified evidence the court learnt that the defendant did not commit an act tht contravene the medical profession especially that of the surgical profession so requires.

The defendant surgeon him self testified that, he has seen that both the liver and the gallbladder was shrank while operating the patient, since the patient's compliant was suffering from sever pain when he ate fatty foods and such a case is the shrinking of the gall bladder from the experience he had gathered for the last 37 years. After discussed and decided with his professional colleagues to remove the gallbladder, he had removed it carefully.

As regards to the removal of the patient's shrank gall bladder so long as the internist proved and referred the patient to the surgeon though, the liver seen shrank the removal of gall bladder can not be presumed as fault. But, the responsibility of the surgeon is not limited to only on the removal of gall bladder and stitch the abdomen. Since the surgeon has found that the patient's liver shrank while operating that was not envisioned prior surgery, he would have done at most due care and follow up what was expected of him after he stitched the abdomen conversely he didn't perform.

Thus according to Art .65 of the Penal Code of Ethiopia will be liable. And also the defendant (surgeon) did not write directives on how to follow up and taking care of the patient on the treatment chart.

There fore, even though efforts have been made by other doctors since the defendant professor Taye Mekuria did not act with due diligence and prudence that the surgical profession so requires after he performed the operation, the patient have died .

52

Thus professor Taye Mekuria is guilty under Art.526 (2) of the penal law of Ethiopia for the imprudent and negligent act.

In the case of Tesfaye vs. professor Taye the court did not raise the legal principles in determining the issue that constitute negligence i.e. Whether the patient has given consent and or informed about the nature of the procedure, common and serious side effects, benefits and reasonable alternatives? And also whether the patient had been informed that the surgery may cause unmanageable bleeding and death. Or the case that the patient died of was remote to foresee.

The usefulness of raising such issues is not about the provision of information but rather the implication is to proof whether there was negligence or the defendant's act was under the circumstances by which a reasonable and careful surgeons perform their obligations.

Never the less, it is common knowledge that the claimant has the burden of alleging and proving the facts of the case that constitute the surgeons fault, it will often found difficult for the patients (the claimant) prosecutor to prove the physicians fault, as it involves more technical matters in to it.

The rational behind for the need to have the body of responsible medical men i.e. like the committee formed by the ministry of health presumably it was meant to provide to court whether the doctor acted in accordance with the practice accepted as proved proper by reasonable body of medical men in that particular art.[19]

Although, the committee have been given reports on issues of the medical profession especially in surgery i.e. what is expected of the surgeon to meet the professional standard with in that specific field. But, the committee in its report did not mention whether any of the information that the prudent patient would want provided sufficiently or not at all, in the light of the medical profession prior surgery.

And also for the defendants to convince the court on the alleged fact i.e. as regards to the amount of information provided to the patient and or omitted to defend have not been raised both by the court and the medical professional committee formed by the ministry of health too.

Be it as it may, whether the committee assumed the right to informed consent is irrelevant or considering it has only minimal effect to the issue and or lack of awareness which may constitute either a battery /Assault/ or negligent, that entails civil and criminal liabilities against the doers on which we will discuss thoroughly hereunder.

As regards to the court, it has had to see whether the legal principle consent preserved, waived by the competent patient himself and or denied by the defendant surgeon prior surgery was not observed and there fore; the right denied with respect to informed consent stated here under:-

What was denied in the litigation here above was that of the major legal principle consent, situated under the Civil Code Of Ethiopia Title XII, Contracts In General, On Art., 1679.[20]

Despite, Ethiopia doesn't have comprehensive and separate medical law for the courts to treat such a case; there is no rule that prevent the judges to analogize from the general contract provision Art. 1679 consent.[21]

But, the reason for the court by then not to observe the legal principle consent was that, presumably (as the writer of this thesis opinion), may be it is due to disregarding the existence of a contractual relation between the patient and the physician.

However, physicians have no obligation to achieve specific result to cure the patient. But, they are duty bound to exercise with due care that meets the professional standard and should not below the care that would be shown in the circumstances by a reasonable, careful physicians i.e. to maintain the legal and ethical principles that the law and profession so requires. Based on the contractual relation they entered to conduct with proper care and skill and as well the law obliged them to keep up informed the patients right to know what is going to happen on his body i.e. the right to informed consent .

It is vital to note that the federal high court was not observed consent that rests on the principle of patient autonomy on its judgment rendered on the 28th of Yekatit 1993, (Penal case no. 3960/88) of the case of Tesfaye vs. professor Taye.

In the case Frehiwot Taddese vs. Dr,Erdaw Ashagare Reta

Frehiwot Tadesse Hospitalized and under treatment in Minilik 2nd Hospital a known oxygen deficient patient on the 10th Tikimt 1994 died from the absence of sufficient oxygen in the hospital.

The defendant Dr. Erdaw Ashagare, who was on duty at the very night when the incident was happened, sued on the grounds for failing to prepare sufficient medical supplies being night duty physician that the profession requires. This failure has caused for the death of Frehiwot, due to oxygen deficiency.

The federal high court criminal bench after adduced evidences expert witnesses adjudged that Dr. Erdaw Ashagare is guilty of negligence for not maintaining the due care and diligence what was expected of himself and of the medical profession under the 1957penal Code Art.526(2)

In the case of Frehiwot vs. Dr. Erdaw Ashagare, however the court proved the defendant is guilty and adjudged the negligent defendant is liable criminally and in the civil suit as well he is civilly liable under Art. 2647(2) of the Civil Code of Ethiopia, for the fault of omission detrimental to the patient.

What civil action taken by the court against the defendant, for not to leave the victim's family remediless was not made known and as well the hospital was not sued vicariously according to Art. 2651 of the civil code of Ethiopia, for the damage caused to the victim by the fault of the hospital's physician.

Pertaining matters related to the civil liability on cases adjudged in the criminal bench. I interviewed Ato Bewnetu Asefa, a judge at the federal first instance court, pertaining the above stated fact and issues related to it and have learnt that although, there are possibilities where issues of civil liabilities could be raised by the claimants to the criminal bench that handled the case, such a case have not been brought to it. Hence, unless, the claimants raise it, the court the court cannot decide on civil liability by its own initiation.

Thus, due to the reason that the claimants didn't raise the issue of civil liability may be of lack of awareness' of the claimants family or of the ignorance of the law on the parts that individual prosecutor who handled the case has caused the unfortunate victims family remediless.

End Notes- Chapter Four

1. Allan   J   Peck,   'Legal   Liabilities'   The   Chartered   Insurance   Institute
    (1991chatamp,Kent)10/8
2. International Encyclopedia Of Medical Law, (1997) Art.161
3. Civil Code Of Ethiopia Proclamation No. 165 Of 1960 Art.2031
4. Ibid
5. Supra Note 2 Art165
6. Ibid
7. The Criminal Code Of Federal Democratic Ethiopia Proclamation
    No.414/2004 Negaret Gazette, (2005) Art.23
8. Supra Note 7 Art,69
9. George Chuhunovich   P11
10. International Encyclopedia Of Medical Law Supra Note 2 Art.170
11. Civil Code Of Ethiopia Proclamation No. 165 Of 1960 Art.2650
12. Supra Note 1at 2/4
13. Supra Note 1 At 2/8
14. Civil Code Of Ethiopia Proclamation No. 165 Of 1960 Art.2651
15. Supra Note 2 Art.174
16. Interview Made With Ato Wubetu Asefa First Instance Court Judge On April
    2007.

Chapter Five Preventive Measures

5.1 Medical Professionals Safe Guard Measure

As we saw in the preceding chapter the day today activities of the medical professionals, is prone ensuing damage/injury or financial loss of individual patients seeking their assistance?

This entails the risk of the medical professionals to be sued for the breach of professional duty or negligent acts, errors or omissions in their professional capacity. As the main purposes of the law is to protect the rights of individual citizens, those unfortunate individuals suffered injury or damage from the negligent acts of the professional would not leave un remedied that is to say that professional is liable for the wrongful act or negligence he/she commit or omit.

Be it as it may, It is very cumbersome for the medical professionals to be liable for cases of negligent act from their pocket, because of the meager financial capacity i.e. skimpy salary they are getting. If this is done with out forethought of such method of a risk transfer, we would be loosing the scanty medical professionals especially doctors i.e. in the country where not more than 2000 doctors are available for about 77,000,000 population. And it may even dissuade the talented individuals to enter in to the profession.

Thus, I propose that one of the possible safe guard measure for the medical professional is professional indemnity insurance which is mainly concerned with the liability of members of learned professions' for injury or damage that the individual patient suffered as a result of breach of professional duty or negligent act .

Pertaining to this matter how ever, the insurance company's here in Ethiopia did not underwrite this class of risk the Ethiopian Insurance Corporation has now a days issued a new policy "professional *indemnity policy medical mal practice insurance"* that was not available previously.

5.2 Clinical Ethics Committee

The first and for most professional safe guard measure is establishing clinical ethics committee that provides ethical support to the medical professionals in many ways one of which is that the committee may discuss cases retrospectively to help identify ethical issues and means to find out the possible solution to them .

The committee as well provides education and training for the medical professionals concerning ethical issues and also it assists in the development of local policies and guidelines by interpreting the national policies in to locally applicable principles.

Thus the existences of the clinical ethics committee refreshes and instill ethical principles in physicians and prevents them from involving in to a negligent act and also keeps the patient from injury or damage.

5.3 Health man power development

With the increased number of population the need for more medical professional is undeniable fact. Thus, seemingly jealously guarded profession that is to say metaphorically "narrow professionalism" or the lesser the concerns of the government health authorities to the health sector.

Be it as it may, the number of the medical professionals, are extremely few to serve the nation. This in turn, has its own unwanted effects even for those who have the chance to see doctors because as the number of doctors are very little and shuttling and working here and there being tiered and fatigue they may involve in to negligent act that may cause to the unfortunate victim to suffer from injury or death.

Thus, it is of paramount importance for the government to strive for more man power development in the health care delivery system through increasing the number of teaching hospitals and intake of increased number of students both by the government itself and encouraging the private investors that deals with medical school. This may alleviate the problems of rush decision making on the patients needs of treatment and the negligent acts of physicians that resulted from being busy working in many places and for more hours a day and at night .

CONCLUSION AND RECOMMENDATIONS

Medical ethics is a branch of ethics. As distinct from the law, that is to say, the legal codes sets a general standard of conduct which must be adhered to civil or criminal consequences, that may fallow for a breach of standards. But in converse, medical ethics however, it is not adopted in to laws and unenforceable, it is the major professional and moral guiding principle which is acquired through interpersonal relation, that infused an innate humanism with axiom "Do No Harm". That can be regarded as a component of moral progress.

This distinction must not regard as expressed, rigid, and sharply differentiated in functions. However, the law and medical ethics are to be perceivable as disciplines with frequent brush in close contact yet each discipline has an exclusive parameter and distinct focal point. Both the medical ethics and the law are share the objective of creating and maintaining societal interest and have the caring tie.

The Professional codes of medical ethics is a quasi judicial in form, and are self-legislative documents developed by a medical profession that can only be enforced by the professionals to attribute to them. In this regard, the health professionals, council of Ethiopia. Regulation No. 76/2002, Art. 16 have endowed with the power and duties to the professional ethics committee to investigate cases for the non observance of professional ethics and after carrying out the investigation on complaints brought against the accused professional, the statement of defense and evidence obtained by committee i.e. the findings with the proposed punishment shall be submitted to the executive committee.

It implies that the medical professionals are duty bound to provide his/her services as to the required ethical standards of behavior and principles diligently, and failure to observe may entail punishments.

In general, both the law and the profession owe to the medical professionals to exercise a high duty of care to their patients and must apply the ordinary degree of professional skill and fallow accepted practice by the profession. In addition, if not exercising such duty of care and prudence that the law requires from an average the professional, entails professional liability (civil and criminal liability). Since Ethiopia does not have medical law that govern the relation between doctors and patient. the civil and criminal liability of the physician for damage or injury caused by improper performance of their duties in the discharge of their his /her professional obligations shall be governed by the traditional civil and criminal law as the rest of the world were using it before the development of the medical law of to date.

How ever, Ethiopia had medical legislation of such kind ever since 18 July 1930s enacted its first modern medical legislation onwards. pieces of medical legislations pertaining registration of medical practitioners, pharmacists and druggists and the proclamation on drug administration and control have been issued, and also there are provisions found here and there that is to say in the Civil Code and Penal Code it could not be assumed that Ethiopia has medical law.

Therefore, the absence of medical law that govern the interactions between doctors and patients; affects a great deal for the lawyers to assist their clients /persons whose right violated by a physician to take his/her case to court and also the judges face problem to decide on cases appeared before court. However they are compelled to pursue the traditional laws .

For instance, ethical principles that involve in the interactions between physician and the patient. Such as, respect for autonomy, beneficence, respect for justice, informed consent, truth telling, confidentiality, respect for man kind and individuals could not be well entertained by the member of the legal profession using the existing civil code, penal code and other pieces of legislation. How ever efforts have been made to grab relevant provision and or analogize for the law not to remain un answerable.

In view of the above analysis, it is imperative to list the following as recommendations.

- It is vital importance the legislatures to draft medical law a discrete area of law concerned with the law governing the interactions between doctors and patients
- Compulsory employer's liability insurance, for both state funded and privately owned health care institution. For the purposes of redress the unfortunate victim . that is to say professional indemnity insurance ,which is mainly concerned with the liability of members of learned professions' for injury or damage that the individual patient suffered as a result of breach of professional duty or negligent act.

62

- Establishing clinical ethics committee/Hospital Ethics Committee/ so as to endow with education and training for the medical professionals regarding ethical issues.
- Government should strive to train more number of medical professionals that can meet the required quality standard especially with more stress on that of doctors.

Bibliography

Table of Books

- Beau champ, Tom L. and Walters. Contemporary issues in Bioethics (Woods
- Worth publishing company, Belmont, California. 3rd ed.1989)
- Beleskaia Natalia. Ethics . (Progress publishers, Moscow, revised ed.1989)
- Brody Howard. ethical decisions in medicine (Little Brown and company, USA. 2nd ed,1981)
- Peck. A. Legal Liabilities. (MacKay's of Chatham plc. ,Chatham Kent Chartered Insurance Institute 1991)
- Pankhurest Richard 'An introduction to the medical history of Ethiopia. (Red Sea Press .1990)
- Powel .A. Liability Insurance .Red wood press Ltd, Mel sham, welt shire. UK. Chartered insurance institute 1992.)
- Spiker Stuart. F and Engelhardt, JR. H. Trisram. Philosophy and medicine .(D. Reidel Publishing Company. Netherlands, vol,3 .1977)
- K Rzeczu nowicz George. Law Of Compensation For Damage. Published By A,A,U 1997)

TABLE OF ARTCLES AND JOURNALS

Good all Jane and B .Elizabeth. Clinical ethics committee Medical Education Resource Africa published by FSG communications limited UK. (2006) volume 28, No 6.

Hope Tony Consent. Medical Education Resource Africa published by FSG communications limited UK. (2006) Volume28, No 6.

Lockwood M. Gillian, Confidentiality. Medical Education Resource Africa published by FSG communications limited UK. (2006) Vol. 28, No 6.

TABLE OF LAWS

- Civil Code Of Ethiopia Proclamation No. 165of 1960 .

- Criminal Code Of Federal Democratic Ethiopia Proclamation No.414/2004 Negarit Gazette,(2005)

- Constitution Of The Federal Democratic Ethiopia, Proclamation No1/1995

- Drug Administration And Control , Proclamation No .176 /1999 Year –Neagret Gazette

- Health Professional Council Regulation No 76 /2002 Year 8 No 13.

- International Encyclopedia Of Medical Law ,(1997)

- Medical Association, Ethiopian. Medical Ethics For <u>Physicians Practicing In Ethiopia</u>. Artistic Printing Enterprise

Website links

- http:/ <u>www.ama</u> assn .org/ ama/ pub/ category/ 2512.html. 2/22/2007

- http:/ www. wma,. net/e/policy/ c8. htm. 2/23/ 2007.

- http: / www. .un .org./over view/rights. Html. 2/23/ 2007

- http/: www. un org./ overview / rights. Html 2/23 /2007

Interviews

- Interview with Dr Yewondwossen Tadesse, Internist, Consultant Nephrologists, Ast. Professor of Internal Medicine, Faculty of Medicine A.A.U .Current Chairman of Ethiopian Medical Association . April, 21, 2007

- Dr, Fetih Yahaya Dr, of chiropractic medicine May ,27 ,2007

- Ato Wubetu Assefa , Judge ,Federal First instance court . April. 27, 2007